THE CROW AND THE PITCHER

Retold by EMMA CARLSON BERNE
Illustrated by TIM PALIN
Music by DEAN JONES

CANTATA
LEARNING

WWW.CANTATALEARNING.COM

CANTATA LEARNING

Published by Cantata Learning
1710 Roe Crest Drive
North Mankato, MN 56003
www.cantatalearning.com

Library of Congress Cataloging-in-Publication Data
Names: Berne, Emma Carlson, author. | Aesop. | Palin, Tim, illustrator.
Title: The crow and the pitcher / retold by Emma Carlson Berne ; illustrated
  by Tim Palin ; music by Dean Jones.
Description: North Mankato, Minnesota : Cantata Learning, [2019] | Series:
  Classic fables in rhythm and rhyme | Summary: A modern song retells the
  fable of the thirsty crow who uses her ingenuity to solve the problem of
  how to drink from a pitcher when the water level is too low. Includes a
  brief introduction to Aesop, sheet music, glossary, discussion questions,
  and further reading. | Includes bibliographical references.
Identifiers: LCCN 2018023445 (print) | LCCN 2018027046 (ebook) | ISBN
  9781684103508 (eBook) | ISBN 9781684103300 (hardcover) | ISBN
  9781684103669 (paperback)
Subjects: LCSH: Children's songs, English--United States--Texts. | CYAC:
  Conduct of life--Songs and music. | Songs. | Fables. | Folklore.
Classification: LCC PZ8.3.B45816 (ebook) | LCC PZ8.3.B45816 Cr 2019 (print) |
  DDC 742.82--dc23
LC record available at https://lccn.loc.gov/2018023445

Book design and art direction: Tim Palin Creative
Editorial direction: Kellie M. Hultgren
Music direction: Elizabeth Draper
Music arranged and produced by Dean Jones

Printed in the United States of America.
0397

This text is set to the tune of "O, Susanna!"

ACCESS THE MUSIC!
SCAN CODE WITH MOBILE APP
CANTATALEARNING.COM

TIPS TO SUPPORT LITERACY AT HOME

WHY READING AND SINGING WITH YOUR CHILD IS SO IMPORTANT

Daily reading with your child leads to increased academic achievement. Music and songs, specifically rhyming songs, are a fun and easy way to build early literacy and language development. Music skills correlate significantly with both phonological awareness and reading development. Singing helps build vocabulary and speech development. And reading and appreciating music together is a wonderful way to strengthen your relationship.

READ AND SING EVERY DAY!

TIPS FOR USING CANTATA LEARNING BOOKS AND SONGS DURING YOUR DAILY STORY TIME

1. As you sing and read, point out the different words on the page that rhyme. Suggest other words that rhyme.

2. Memorize simple rhymes such as Itsy Bitsy Spider and sing them together. This encourages comprehension skills and early literacy skills.

3. Use the questions in the back of each book to guide your singing and storytelling.

4. Read the included sheet music with your child while you listen to the song. How do the music notes correlate to the words of the song?

5. Sing along on the go and at home. Access music by scanning the QR code on each Cantata book. You can also stream or download the music for free to your computer, smartphone, or mobile device.

Devoting time to daily reading shows that you are available for your child. Together, you are building language, literacy, and listening skills.

Have fun reading and singing!

Aesop was a storyteller who wrote hundreds of stories called **fables**. These stories often have animals for characters. Each short story is meant to teach a **moral**, or lesson.

In this fable, a thirsty crow tries to get a drink of water from a deep **pitcher**. But she can't reach the water! How does she solve her problem? Read and sing along to find out!

The day was hot. The crow was, too.

A pitcher stood nearby.

"Water, please," the poor crow thought,

"or oh, I just might cry."

The pitcher held some water cool,

but only way down deep.

The crow tried hard to take a sip,

but her beak just wouldn't reach.

When you have a problem,
don't just sit and cry.
Look hard to find an answer.
You'll see one if you try.

She reached in from the left and right
and even from the air.
She twisted, turned, and **jammed**
her beak as far down as she dared.

But that pitcher was too deep.

She flapped away so sad.

Then, as she spied a pile of rocks,

a clever thought she had.

When you have a problem,
don't just sit and cry.
Look hard to find an answer.
You'll see one if you try.

The crow picked up a little rock
and held it in her beak.
She dropped it in the pitcher with a
plinkety-plink-plink-plink.

In she tossed another rock
and another the same way.
She worked so hard that she just knew
she'd have a drink that day.

When you have a problem,
don't just sit and cry.
Look hard to find an answer.
You'll see one if you try.

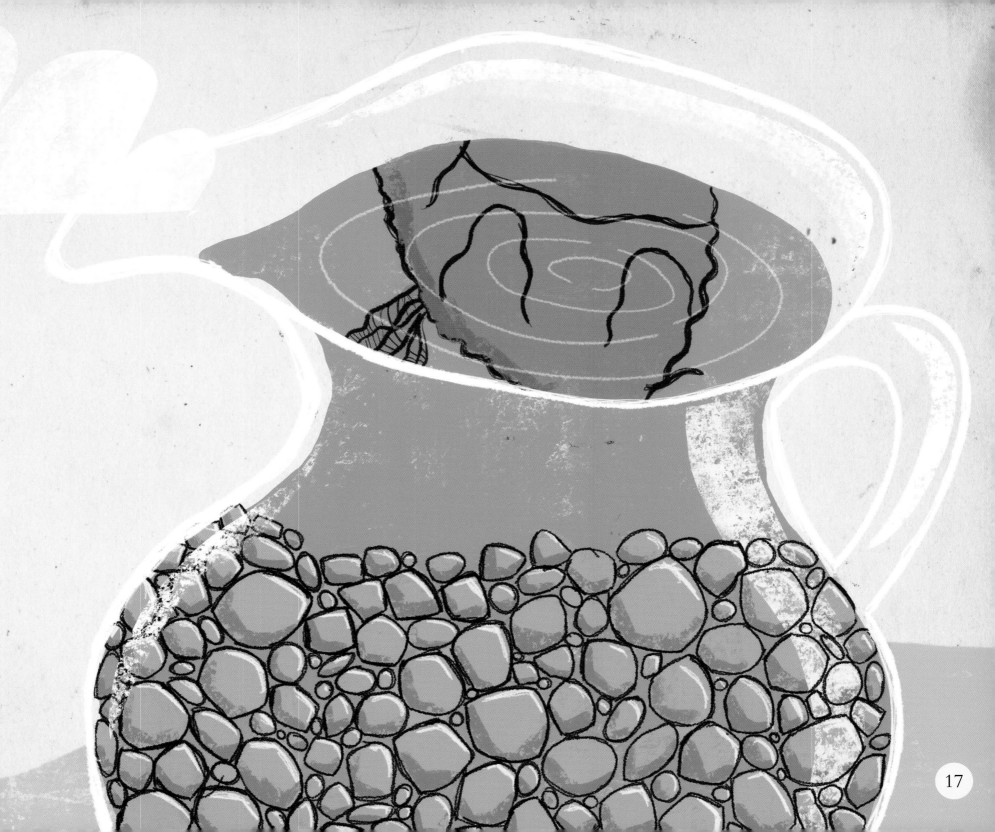

As she piled the rocks inside,
the water rose up high.
At last it reached the pitcher's **rim**.
The crow let out a sigh.

"I helped myself. I didn't quit.
I took some time to think.
Now it's time for my **reward**."
And that crow, she took a drink.

When you have a problem,
don't just sit and cry.
Look hard to find an answer.
You'll see one if you try.